Praise for, "The Young Entrepreneur's Guide to Success 2.0," and Sylvester Chisom's Speaking Engagements

"Sylvester, go and touch the world with your book. They need it!"
-Dr. Cathy Ashmore
Founder, Consortium for Entrepreneurship Education

"It was a true honor to meet you. What an incredible person you are! Your book is an easy read for young entrepreneurs."
-Steve Mariotti
Founder, NFTE (Network For Teaching Entrepreneurship)

"I was truly impressed with your presentation. The learning that is in the book can be directly applied to India. I am very happy to take these concepts back to India and apply them at my University there."
-Priyank Narayan
Founder, IndiaPreneurship
New Delhi, India

"Congrats on your new book! Wishing you continued success."
Jeff Hoffman
Founder, Priceline.com

"I was fortunate to visit with Sylvester. He is dynamic!"
-Linda Krehbiel
Director, MO DESE Business, Marketing & Information Technology

"I am very impressed with, "The Young Entrepreneur's Guide to Success 2.0." We will use the book in an adolescent teen pregnancy group, state youth detention, a homeless shelter, our summer youth camp, and at a local Delaware school."
-Ronni K. Cohen
Executive Director, Delaware Financial Literacy Institute

"Sylvester, you were terrific. Our students and staff really enjoyed your presentation."
-Tim Murrell
Director of Career Tech Education, St. Louis Public Schools

"I greatly enjoyed your session and am loving going through your book! I have already shared it with several colleagues."
-Matthew Thompson
Program Director, National Lemonade Day

THE YOUNG ENTREPRENEUR'S GUIDE TO SUCCESS

2.0

8 LESSONS TO LAUNCH YOUR BIG IDEA

Sylvester Chisom

With Jameka Merriweather

BOOKS FROM SPEAKER AND BEST SELLING AUTHOR SYLVESTER CHISOM

The Young Entrepreneur's Guide to Success
10 Lessons To Build Business Savvy

The Young Entrepreneur's Guide to Success 2.0
8 Lessons To Launch Your Big Idea

About The Author

Sylvester Chisom is a nationally respected entrepreneurship expert, speaker, and author whose books are used in high school and college classrooms across the country. He has been featured in The Wall Street Journal, The Globe & Mail Canada, worldnews.com and more. He co-founded Showroom Shine Express Detailing at the young age of 18 with only a water hose, a bucket, and a dream. This young entrepreneur has won the prestigious Steve Harvey Neighborhood Award four years in a row for his company's entrepreneurial contribution to the community. Each year Sylvester speaks in person and online at high schools, colleges, organizations, and conferences. He shares his personal stories and helpful strategies to find success through entrepreneurship. To date he has reached more than a million aspiring entrepreneurs and counting.

For more Information on books or booking Sylvester to speak:

Booking@sylvesterchisom.com

Sylvesterchisom.com

Social Media

As the founder of theyounginc.com, Sylvester has created a social network for young entrepreneurs and entrepreneurial thinkers from around the world to connect, learn, and share ideas. Join the movement!

Twitter: @mrchisom   Facebook: sylvesterchisom

JAMEKA MERRIWEATHER BIO

Jameka Merriweather is a goal oriented young lady bent upon fulfilling her God-given purpose throughout her hometown of St. Louis, Mo. She is a member of Delta Sigma Theta Sorority, Inc., where she was given the name "Freedom Writer." As a child she won the *Dr. Martin Luther King I Have A Dream Speech Essay Contest* and as an adult, she was awarded by the Houston Association of Black Journalists. She has been published in the Suburban Journals, the Black College Wire, as well as the first Young Entrepreneurs' guide to success. Jameka holds a Bachelor of Arts in Communication from Prairie View University and is currently pursuing a Masters in Education from Lindenwood University.

Jameka is enthralled by coaching and mentoring today's youth. She is a track coach for the Royal Knights Athletic Association and a cheerleading coach for both Hazelwood East Middle and Trinity Catholic High Schools. Jameka continues her drive to reach the younger generation as a Sunday school teacher, Church School teacher, and one of the Youth Gospel Night Chairpersons at First Missionary Baptist Church of Kinloch in Black Jack.

Jameka, continues to pursue freelance writing opportunities and aspires to publish enough books to fill a small bookcase.

<u>Connect with Jameka:</u>
j.merriweather@att.net
Twitter:@merri_jaye
Facebook: Merri.Jaye

THE YOUNG ENTREPRENEUR'S GUIDE TO SUCCESS 2.0

Sylvester Chisom

With Jameka Merriweather

© 2013 Young Entrepreneur Publishing Group

PRINTED IN THE UNITED STATES

ISBN: 978-0-615-92021-4

FIRST EDITION: NOVERMBER 2013

For special quantity discounts for bulk purchases:

YEPUBLISHING@GMAIL.COM

COVER DESIGN BY: Halle Malcomb

TABLE OF CONTENTS

A message to the reader   1

1. Raising the expectations of you   2

2. Limitless success   14

3. Create a movement   25

4. Get funded   40

5. Run a lean business   54

6. The social media advantage   68

7. Develop a winning business model   84

8. 30 days to launch manual   102

    Young Entrepreneur Resources   107

A Message To The Reader

My mission is to help you realize your full potential and make the impact in the world you were created to make. No matter your given circumstances or struggles believe you can overcome those. You are unconquerable. You were born with a genius level skill or talent. It is your duty to find out what that is and develop it. The world needs you. It needs that big idea that you've been dreaming about. Whether you are launching a brand new business or taking your existing company to the next level, this book is here to inspire you and help turn your big idea into a profitable reality.

BE GREAT!

-Sylvester Chisom

@mrchisom

Chapter 1

RAISING THE EXPECTATIONS OF YOU

"I HATED EVERY MINUTE OF TRAINING,

BUT I SAID 'DON'T QUIT.

SUFFER NOW AND

LIVE THE REST OF YOUR LIFE

LIKE A CHAMPION!' "

-MUHAMMED ALI

Imagine this, two 18 year old high school boys with a water hose, a bucket, and a dream of starting a carwash business. For me this is how I first got my feet wet as a young entrepreneur. It was a cold winter day in the back parking lot of my mother's hair salon, Professional Touch in St. Louis, Mo. My story goes like this, after working for a local car wash chain, my best friend Arthur and I realized an underserved niche in the industry. We noticed there were some customers who wanted a more detailed cleaning and would pay more to get it. As ambitious high school kids we figured out a way to provide that detailed service and make money while doing it.

A passion from within drove us to build what is now known as, Showroom Shine Express Detailing. In 2013, that desire continues to push us passed perceived barriers, limitations, and excuses. We are never complacent with our success. Thus, we continue to raise the expectations of ourselves.

The key to any success is the foundation. As a young entrepreneur, that foundation begins with you. When I wrote my first book, "The Young Entrepreneur's Guide to Success," my company had one location and had been voted the nation's Best Detailing Shop by the Steve

Harvey Neighborhood Awards. Today as you read my second book, "The Young Entrepreneur's Guide to Success 2.0," the first book is being used in high schools and colleges; I speak at schools and conferences across the country; one location has turned into three; Showroom Shine has four consecutive awards as the Steve Harvey Neighborhood Awards Best Detail Shop winner; we have been featured in the Wall Street Journal; and I have been recognized in Ebony Magazine as one of the top young entrepreneurs in the nation. In my mind, there is always so much more to achieve, another idea to develop, one more business to launch. Train yourself to think this way.

You must understand that opportunities build off each other. One success or failure will create another opportunity to grow. Always continue to raise the expectations of yourself, your team, and your business as you move forward.

"Sometimes when you innovate, you make mistakes. It is best to admit them quickly, and get on with improving your other innovations."
-Steve Jobs

Ok, so it's easy to say, stay innovative and always look for more opportunities to improve your business. That is great advice, but you may say to yourself, well how? How do I continue to push myself? It is all about having the right mindset. I have developed three P's to developing a winning mentality. There are 3 key components that affect your ability to remain in drive versus falling in neutral, or even worse, reverse.

3 P's to developing a winning mentality

1. Perseverance

Loving your business when loving your business matters the most...

When the fun part is over, when the new car smell has worn off, when the excitement begins to dwindle, the first reaction is to run. The first reaction is to give up and close up shop, for good. Research from the U.S. Bureau of Labor Statistics suggests that most failures of American businesses will occur within the first two years of their existence.

Your name in lights sounds good but doing the work now to be a champion later may not sound so appealing. When it's hard to see the success in your future, remember your vision statement. In my first book, there is a chapter about developing a vision statement (creating a clear vision of the experience, look, feel, smell, and sound) of your business. It should be something forward looking that your company is working toward. When it is hard to see the light at the end of the tunnel, refer back to your vision statement to refocus and propel you through the difficult times. Ask yourself, "What's next?"

Moving forward boils down to one word: Innovation. Your business is a living organism; treat it as such. Your business must grow. Your business must thrive. Your business must pivot. In the fast pace business environment we live in today, there is a need to continually search for ways to refresh your business and break new ground. Look for ways to improve. Search for new markets to penetrate. It may be as simple as making your website more user-friendly, but it maintains the idea of staying fresh and new. Innovation is not just for practice but let it become an important part of the culture of your business.

---

2. **P**reparation

It's Your Time to S.H.I.N.E

> *"The way to climb a mountain is*
> *one step at a time."*
> *-@mrchisom*

You want to create achievable short-term goals that eventually will result in accomplishing the long-term goal. Continuous goal setting is a major factor in remaining innovative and raising the expectations of what you are able to achieve. The best part about goal setting, is when you reach the small moments of achievement you celebrate them!

You may read this and say, I know I need goals but how do I effectively form one? How do I execute on that goal? When you think about goal setting have a winning mentality and tell yourself, "It is my time to shine!" To keep you inspired along your journey we have created what we call "S.H.I.N.E" goals. You have to remain in a state of preparedness and this method is what we use to create and stay focused on a goal.

"S.H.I.N.E" GOALS

Simplify: Long-term goals should break down into small steps. Create a small attainable goal that is straightforward and easy to accomplish. The goal should be something that once completed you will be closer to achieving your long term goal. This will get you headed in the right direction. Accomplishing the small goals will keep you encouraged.

How: This is the planning phase. Now it is time to set your timeline and your plan of action. Write down the tasks you will do to reach your goal. Set a deadline for when you will complete each task.

Initiate: Now, put your plan into action. You have a well thought out plan with deadlines and it is time to act. If you said you would talk to 10 potential customers before the end of the month, start making those calls.

Navigate: Understand you will meet obstacles on your pathway to successfully achieving your goal. You are the driver and you are in control. Be flexible enough to take alternative routes to achieving the tasks required to reach your goal. You may have to take a detour and pivot in order to overcome a challenge.

Evaluate: Review your progress and success at the deadline that you have set. Did you reach your goal? If not be realistic, you may have to change some steps in your plan or increase your timeframe. What feedback did you get? Use the feedback to make revisions to your plan. You may learn that you need to pivot and set a new goal. It is ok; remember goal setting is a continuous process.

---

3. **P**ositivity

Healthy is Wealthy

As a young entrepreneur, you are not awarded a bank full of sick days and you want to do your best to remain in good health. Be conscious of your mental, physical, and spiritual health. You want to keep yourself centered, focused, and calm. It is easier to make good decisions when you have inner peace.

It is recommended you manage stress levels by implementing one of the following techniques, meditation, deep breathing, or yoga to name a few. The best time to use one of these techniques or one of your own is in the morning; it is the part of the day you have the most control over. How you start your day has a huge impact on your daily productivity. It is also important to remember to eat right and give your body the proper fuel it needs.

During the day, you may want to implement an exercise routine. Physical fitness allows time to clear your thoughts and ease your mind, sort of an oasis away from the worries of the world. Creates your "me time" to zone out, listen to music and release all of the stress endorphins from the day.

All of these practices ignite a happier, healthier you. When you are happy, you exude positive energy that is

> *I have meditated for years. It has given me energy, strength, health, wisdom, and access to my own inner stillness, inner silence, and inner bliss. It is my connection to myself; it is my connection to the universe.*
> *-Russell Simons*

essential to your business success. Your employees and customers will follow your lead and feed off your positive energy. Your surroundings should mirror your effort to resonate positivity and if it does not change it. As the leader of your business, you are the core. When you are off centered, your business could be impacted negatively.

Do your best to create a culture filled with the positive energy you want to see. Maintaining a healthy diet and finding constructive methods to manage your stress will also help you stay on the right track and moving in the right direction. Healthy is wealthy. Keep all these principles in mind as you set out to launch your big idea and achieve great things.

Launch Activity 1:

Define your business idea that you are preparing to launch. Refer to the S.H.I.N.E. goal methodology throughout the process of developing your idea into a winning business.

IDEA DEVELOPMENT

Passion
What are 3 things you are passionate about?
1)
2)
3)

Talent
What are 3 things you feel like you do better than anyone else — what activities do you feel like you were just "made to do"?
1)
2)
3)

Niche
Have you noticed an area in life that you feel like something is missing or could be better?
1)
2)
3)

Don't reinvent the wheel

What are 3 businesses that you have seen you would be interested in trying?

1)

2)

3)

What is your business idea?

What makes economic sense — how can you create a business to make money combining your passion and talent?

_____

_____

_____

_____

_____

_____

_____

Chapter 2

LIMITLESS SUCCESS

"THERE ARE NO

LIMITATIONS

TO THE MIND

EXCEPT

THOSE WE ACKNOWLEDGE."

-Napolean Hill

What are limits?

Limits are barriers you place on yourself!
When I met Dave Stewart, founder of World Wide
Technology, the idea of a mindset of limitless success was
brought to the forefront. Stewart shared how he remained
hungry for continued growth as a businessman. As the
founder of the largest black owned company in America
(4.1 billion dollars in sales in 2011), Stewart pushes the
"limits." During our time together, Stewart told a story
about visiting a historic Wall Street bank in New York.
While meeting with the CEO of the bank, Stewart said he
inquired about the daily dollar amount of transactions
processed at the bank.

The CEO told him over a trillion dollars worth of
transactions are exchanged daily at the bank. Stewart said
for him that meant there was another level of business out
there. He said after that meeting he asked his self the
question, "What portion of those transactions do I want to
be mine?" He further commented that it made him realize
even though he was running a multibillion dollar a year
business that he could do so much more. He understood he
needed to remove the limits off his way of thinking.

Again, limits are barriers you place on yourself.
Ask yourself at its greatest point, what does your big idea

look like? Who are the customers of your business? How much revenue does your business generate? How many people do you employ? How many locations do you have? How many subscribers does your website have? Now, remove the limitations off your dreams and way of thinking and ask yourself those same questions. Think big, no bigger. It may sound cliché' but "the possibilities are endless." As a leader you must first believe that.

Although the limits are only mental barriers, you have to be willing to put your genius level talent to work. Ultimately this is what ends up creating limitless success.

> *"Hide not your talents. They for use were made. What's a sundial in the shade?"*
> -Benjamin Franklin

Limitless Revenue –"A Blank Check"

Imagine you have a check written out to you, signed, and ready to go. The only information that is missing is the dollar amount. What amount would you write in this blank?

Did you say 10 million, a billion, or a trillion dollars? Well that is up to you. There is no wrong amount to fill in. That is totally up to you. The blank check is a symbol for you to expand the way you think about your financial potential. It is important to put an amount and a date. The date will help to give you a time frame to work within.

Whatever level you are currently thinking on now, take it up to the next level. When you work for an employer and you earn $9.50 an hour, you are sure that no matter how much extra money you make the company, your hourly gain will still be $9.50 an hour. But, as an entrepreneur, once you remove the limits on your financial potential, how much you make depends on how much financial success you achieve with your company. Every time you look at your business, you should see an open door to the bank where your account is limitless, your revenue is limitless, and your potential is limitless.

Limitless Satisfaction – "Be Hungry"

Just like Dave Stewart, you should never be content with the current state of your business. You should always be analyzing your business to determine who else you can touch, what other market you can reach, where else in the world can you have an impact. Do not be afraid to pivot and evolve.

Let us take a look at the hotel giant Marriott International. Do you know what connection they have with A & W Root Beer? The Marriott hotels started from an A & W Root Beer stand. Yet, armed with the idea that any business venture is limitless, founder Mr. J. Willard Marriott can pivot from quenching peoples thirst with root beer stands to creating one of the largest and most powerful hospitality brands across the globe. It all comes down to the Marriott brand having a relentless focus on innovation and action.

At the heart of the entrepreneurial spirit is innovation. Great entrepreneurs are never satisfied and are always looking to create something new, make something better, and add more value. There is always an idea that can be improved upon. The cell phone did not evolve into a calendar, camera, camcorder, PDA, and personal assistant by someone being content with huge car phones that could not leave an automobile. Take a look at your cell phone and see the power of limitless innovation in action.

You must remain hungry for improvement.

> **"There's a way to do it better...find it."**
>
> - Thomas Edison

Limitless Mindset
"Control the Way You Think"

The biggest barriers are mental barriers – limits. The moment you are faced with a roadblock in your business, you begin to place limitations on your success. The problem in itself becomes a limitation. First, focus on the solution not the problem. You can worry about the problem all day long but it will not resolve itself. As soon as you are faced with a problem, begin brainstorming ideas to combat the problem.

Problem: My advertising campaign isn't working.

Limited Thinking

Advertising doesn't work for my business.

Limitless Thinking

I will brainstorm with my team about where our target market goes to find our type of product or service. We will make sure we are visible there. I will think outside of the box and find more targeted approaches to reach my customers. I will try a mix of traditional media (radio and newspaper) with nontraditional approaches (Google Adwords, blogging, Facebook and twitter ads).

Now, you have controlled the way you addressed the problem and developed a solution. Each problem you encounter has the ability to be a set back or a set up for you to derive a plan of action and overcome it. Put your plan into action.

----

4 Tips to a Limitless Mindset

1) **Ask yourself, "Is my thinking limited?"** This will help you to seek greater possibilities when making decisions.

2) **Ask yourself "What's next?"** You are not defined by your past. Whether the past was good or bad continue to tell yourself that your greatest days are still ahead of you.

3) **Take a deep breath.** Sometimes a pause will help us see the solutions more clearly. This will help you to not feed into the sometimes unnecessary pressure or time restraints we put on ourselves.

4) **Be open-minded to change.** A good pivot could unlock the limitless potential you have been waiting on. Don't be afraid, embrace change.

Ultimately, your big idea can be as successful as you dare it to be. Every business starts with a thought, a seed. It's up to the leaders to grow that idea and tap into the business' limitless potential. The great entrepreneurs remain hungry for improvements to their businesses. Adapt this way of thinking as you move forward with your company. Remember, the purpose of limitless thinking is to create an expanded mindset. You want a mindset where you are not holding back your success with narrow-minded or negative thinking. Write out your blank check and use it as a symbol to remind you that you control the key to your financial potential. Keep your mind focused on achieving limitless success.

Launch Activity 2

1) Read the story about Dave Steward taking the limits off his business potential. Take a moment to reflect on your current business idea and how can it be bigger or make a greater impact. Write down a bigger version of your original idea.

_____

_____

_____

_____

_____

_____

_____

2) Write down any perceived barriers that you feel may stop you from success. For each barrier, write down a positive solution to overcome it.

_____

_____

_____

_____

_____

_____

_____

3) Fill out the blank check with an amount of money you desire to have. Also assign a date to when you want to have this amount. Finally write down what are you willing to sacrifice to achieve this amount.

5284

PAY TO THE
ORDER OF _____ $ [   ]

_____ DOLLARS

FOR _____

⑈2222222 ⑆ 123 111 555⑈ 5284

_____

_____

_____

_____

_____

Chapter 3

CREATE A MOVEMENT

"WHEN THE YOUTH OF AMERICA

GET TOGETHER,

AMAZING THINGS HAPPEN."

-TOM FORD

On June 29, 2007 Apple released the first generation iPhone and effectively changed the way we viewed our cell phones. Phones before the iPhone were primarily for calling, texting, and if you really had to you could browse the web and send an email. By introducing the idea of the app and all touch screen interface Apple molded the future of the smart phone and also led to the emergence of all-in-one PC's and tablets. With people crowding Apple stores at the introduction of each new version of the iPhone it is safe to say Apple created a movement.

A movement brings people together. A movement pushes people to action. A movement in business is customer centered, not product centered. You must get customers to follow your business because you do an amazing job at solving a problem for them. If your business becomes a movement it will effectively change some aspect of people's lives. You don't want to be just another business. The ultimate expression of a business is for it to become a movement. Amazon is a movement. Apple is a movement. Facebook and Twitter are movements. You should work to develop your business into a movement. How though? How did those businesses set the foundation to create a movement instead of creating a less impactful business? There are three keys.

- ❖ **Branding**
- ❖ **Collaboration**
- ❖ **Explosive Growth**

❖ Branding

Thus far, we have talked about what your business looks like to you but one of the most important ways to set your business apart from other businesses is having a strong brand identity. From a customer's point of view what is the experience like with your business? It is important to be aware that you control all of the contact points between your business and your customers:

- ✓ What does your business feel like?
- ✓ What does it look like?
- ✓ How does it smell?
- ✓ What is the web experience like?
- ✓ What type of impression does it leave on the customer?
- ✓ Is it memorable?

If there are 50,000 ecommerce clothing websites in the world, what sets your business apart from the other 49,999? Your brand should make it as easy as possible for your customers to think of your business in a positive manner. Although your name and logo are important, your brand is bigger than just that. Your brand is the total representation of the idea. When everything is put together, what does it create?

Think of Twitter, What is the user experience like on a mobile device vs. a laptop?

The user experience is consistent in both experiences. Consumers expect that.

Think of Nike. What does it represent?

Athletes, winning, sports...you may see the Nike swoosh but overall your thoughts are winners and great athletes. The Nike logo has a clear identity.

Think of McDonald's. What do you taste?

Regardless of which McDonald's in the world you visit, you taste the same Big Mac. The product is consistent customers expect that.

Think of Gatorade. What do you feel?

You may feel replenished and your thirst is now quenched. The product delivers on what it tells its customers it represents.

These are four major brands and what do they all have in

common? Their brand identities are bold, consistent and simple. Whatever your brand represents should be a clear and fearless idea. In this day and age, business moves at a very fast pace.

A smart brand remains true to its identity and utilizes the modern communications of the times to share that information. It is important to be where the people are to maximize your exposure. If "the people" are on Facebook, Twitter, Instagram, Pinterest, etc you should consider how these communication outlets can help you to better brand your business.

Speaking of Instagram, Instagram as a business exemplifies the very idea of a simple and bold brand concept. The initial idea founder Kevin Sytstrom had for the business that would eventually become Instagram was an app called Burbn. It would be a place for social networking, gaming, photos, and a host of other initiatives. But he soon realized the photo portion was receiving the most attention. So he changed the name to Instagram, the business idea was scaled down to something clear and bold, photos. Amazingly just 18 months after launching Instagram was acquired by Facebook for 1 billion dollars. What is the lesson to be learned? Your brand cannot represent everything; create a clear and bold concept, then run with it.

■ *Re-Branding*

So, we know that branding is important but there may come a time when *re-branding* is just as important. Take the Penn State Jerry Sandusky scandal or BP after the massive 2010 Gulf of Mexico oil spill. Both organizations faced critical periods and a need to re-invent their image and rebuild their brand with the public. Penn State was known to stand for integrity and honor. Now, they will have to rebuild their brand for it to be identified in that same light by the public. The branding lesson to be learned is to protect the integrity of your brands image.

After the 2010 Gulf of Mexico oil spill, BP made sure to display great works with charities and community involvement in the gulf coast. They had to show the public that they still cared about the community. BP has set aside 42 billion dollars for the total potential tab.

Athletes and celebrities, re-brand from time to time. It doesn't necessarily have to be a negative event that causes a movement of re-branding but it may be time to shake things up. Sean "P. Diddy" Combs hip hop mogul is a good example of re-branding simply to keep things fresh. The Marquee Blog via CNN Entertainment reports Combs as saying, *"I've gone as Puff, Puffy, Puff Daddy, P. Diddy, Diddy, King Combs – my real name is Sean Combs –*

and for a week, this week only, you can call me by my new name, Swag." Combs likes to have fun and change his name to go with the times. Again, we're in a fast-paced society. Re-branding is one way to keep up. When the business is slow or the product no longer meets the needs of the consumers, it may be a good time to reevaluate your brand.

Now you should understand the idea of a brand but it may still be kind of foggy as to *why* it's so important. Yeah, it'll distinguish my business but what does it *really* do in the big picture, in the grand scheme of things? It creates credibility! Consumers do business with businesses they are familiar with and that they like. They go to the names they know and trust, and are willing to pay for it.

> *"Price is what you pay.*
> *Value is what you get"*
> *-Warren Buffett*

Just like the Nike swoosh and Warren Buffett's quote, what your brand represents should create value with your consumers. So when other products are presented to them, their heart beats to the beat of your drum. In their minds, they are already sold on what your brand represents. Branding is a major component in developing your business into a movement.

❖ Collaboration

Create something greater together. You want to grow your business but you cannot do it alone. Being an entrepreneur is not a game of horseshoes, it's not an individual sport; it's a team sport. You may have a great product or service but someone else may have an underserviced customer base that could benefit from your product. Why spin your wheels when part of the work is already done for you? The best reason to partner with other businesses, vendors, and partners simply put is because it will help you to move faster and more efficiently.

Give a little to make a lot. Owning 100% of nothing will always get you 100% of nothing but, 30% of a lot will look much better in your bank account. Our Parking Spot airport carwash locations represent a partnership to reach an underserved niche of people who want the convenience of having the car washed while they park at the airport. Our car detailing business gained access to a new customer base and The Parking Spot added greater value to their parking customers. It's a great example of collaboration.

In the spirit of remaining hungry, you always want to reach out to new markets and in doing so; it will help to have experienced contacts in the areas you want to reach. Reaching out to new markets creates those avenues and networks you'll need to expand and grow. If you're good at singing but you know someone who is good at playing the drums and someone who is good at playing the keyboard and another person can play a mean bass guitar. Put everyone together and you've got a band. You do what you are good at and let other people do what they are good at. Together you all can create beautiful music.

How to Evaluate a Good Partner

Okay, so your friend may have a skill that can be used to help your business but will that partnership truly be beneficial to the success of your company? Here are some questions to ask of potential partners.

- ✓ Do you share common values and beliefs?
- ✓ How will you deal with conflict?
- ✓ Do you possess similar work ethic?
- ✓ How fast do you want the business to grow?
- ✓ Do you have a clear vision for the partnership and a definite exit strategy?

How To Be A Better Partner

You may have an excellent idea, but are you a good partner? There are some key objectives to keep in mind when you evaluate yourself as a business partner.

- ✓ Be upfront and honest about your needs and expectations.
- ✓ Remain open minded to your partner's ideas, and also their opportunities for improvement.
- ✓ Stay clear on how the partnership benefits your business objectives.
- ✓ Understand the terms of the agreement and abide by those terms.

❖ Explosive Growth

How to Scale your Business

One of the key evaluations of your collaboration is how fast you want your business to grow. I have outlined 4 simple ideas that can assist in creating explosive growth of your business.

1. You need operating Leverage

Your business will not scale if your revenue grows at the same rate of your operating costs. At some point, your revenue intake needs to outperform the cost it takes to create additional revenue for the business. Your operating costs increase should grow at a slower rate than your revenue over time. If you add 3 employees which generate more revenue but it costs just as much to pay those employees, then you have defeated the purpose and added no dollars to your businesses profit. If you add 3 employees, the revenue they create should outpace the cost to employ them. The rate that your revenue grows over time should grow faster than the rate that your cost grows overtime.

2. Streamline Basic Process

Your most basic processes should be repeatable and teachable. Streamline those processes so that you can easily train someone else to do it. The other skills that require more expertise will require more training.

Here is a simple example, @ShowroomShine has a streamlined process for washing cars that can be taught easily to workers but the, "final check" requires more skill and training before it is mastered. The basic processes, washing, vacs, waxing,etc. are structured so the managers are not confined to those tasks. When you are able to hand off structured tasks to other team members, it will free your time to complete other tasks requiring more specialized skills.

3. Work ON Your Business Not IN Your Business

Now, you have all the free time in the world to just sit back and twiddle your thumbs right? Wrong. It is important to spend time on improving your company. This step requires you to step away from the daily operation of the business. Working on your business means that you are fine tuning the concept and doing the things that will help it grow and expand. When you are not locked down with the daily operation you can focus on the engines of growth for your business. For example, meeting with potential clients, developing new markets, increasing the impact of your brand, attending networking events – all tasks that will essentially grow your business.

4. Have Financial Stability For Expansion

The previous three concepts are important but at the root of the business is money, funding. In order to keep growing your business, you should be securing funding to be able to expand. Line up investors for backing or boot strap as far as you can by reinvesting your profits into the business. You can have the best idea in the world, but without the funds to see that idea through that is all you have, an idea.

Keep these concepts in mind and how they should be implemented into your business as you grow. From time to time go back and read this chapter again for motivation. If these concepts are executed and applied correctly you may have a chance of creating a company that changes the way people do things. Ultimately you could the next person to turn your big idea into a movement, the ultimate expression of a business.

Launch Activity 3

Branding

In a simple, bold, consistent way, what does your brand represent?

_____

_____

_____

How does your brand add value to customer's lives?

_____

_____

_____

Collaboration

What values should you and your business partners share?

_____

_____

_____

What 3 things can you do to make yourself a better partner?

_____

_____

_____

Explosive Growth

What basic processes in your business can be streamlined?

_____

_____

_____

Evaluate your business processes to see if it will scale. Does your revenue grow at the same rate as your operating costs?

_____

_____

_____

Chapter 4

GET FUNDED

"ALWAYS CHOOSE YOUR INVESTORS

BASED ON WHO YOU WANT TO WORK WITH,

BE FRIENDS WITH, AND GET ADVICE FROM.

NEVER, EVER,

CHOOSE YOUR INVESTORS

BASED ON VALUATION."

-JASON GOLDBERG, FAB

So far so good, right? You have clarity on your big idea, and you are preparing for limitless success. Well, here is the kicker. In order to run a successful business, you need money. Most businesses fail because there was not enough working capital to maintain the business. Initially, when you start your business it will take time for the business to reach a point of profitability. Your business will need funding in order to be able to maintain until it is generating enough revenue to take care of itself. In order for your big idea to achieve maximum success it must make it through these stages of development. Different types of funding are appropriate at each point.

In a nutshell, why do you need funding?

❖ **Start Up**
- How much money do you need to get started?

❖ **Operation**
- Working capital for daily expenses, tools, marketing, maintenance, employees, etc.

❖ **Expansion**
- New markets, countries, customer segments, technology, developing products, etc.

❖ Exit

- Sell the company to an acquirer or leads to an IPO

Types of Funding

■ Bootstrapping

Every founder will not agree to seek out funding right away and may choose, "bootstrapping" the process where you use your own money and labor to fund the company. Truth be told, this is probably how you will start. This option will do three things: Preserve ownership for the founders, force you to run a lean business, and help stimulate creativity. Many companies start this way until it is absolutely necessary to seek funding. In most cases this is usually how an idea gets off the ground.

For example, in 2008 the company WooThemes (woothemes.com) was founded and bootstrapped to success by three young entrepreneurs, Adii Pienaar, Mark Forrester, and Magnus Jepson. They grew the company organically, from a humble beginning selling only a handful of commercial WordPress themes. They now offer a huge catalog of feature rich themes and a suite of plugins that extend the WordPress experience. Today, WooThemes has over 40,000 users and more than 1.8 million downloads, generating over $2 million in revenue. In an online interview, founder Pienaar says, "With WooThemes we're trying to find that balance between financial ambition and the happiness that WooThemes creates in our individual lives." Keep in mind as your company grows that founder happiness should be taken into consideration as you choose how to fund your big idea.

■ Friends and Family

Tap into your personal network. When my business partner Arthur and I founded Showroom Shine Express Detailing and needed startup money, it was my mom providing a $500 loan to get the ball rolling. We were able to obtain equipment needed to generate money. Initially most of the money made was reinvested back into the business to help it grow. By using friends and family as funding sources, you may be able to negotiate better terms as far as repaying a loan or giving them a small piece of ownership in the business. If it is a loan, there may be little to no interest to repay the loan. Also in most cases the investment or loan is usually based more on your personal relationship versus qualifications such as credit, income, or other financial standings.

Although it may be one of the easiest routes of funding, be mindful of mixing your personal and professional relationships. The agreement will probably be based on personal feelings and you will have to honor those relationships throughout the terms of the loan. You do not want to damage a personal relationship with a friend or family member based on a bad business deal.

■ Angel Investors

Angel investors are wealthy individuals who have the funds to invest in early stage or start-up companies and usually thrive off the idea of helping a new business. There are established angel investor groups and there are also angel investors who will take some research to find.

Some established angel investors across the country include The New York Angels of New York City, CommonAngels of Lexington, Massachusetts, Bob Geras of Chicago, IL, and the Angel's Forum of Palo Alto, California. Angels in America has some common angel investor profiles and links to their websites. Angel List is a great resource for startups to find investors as well as a good place to meet talent. (www.angel.co)

Other angel investors may require networking with other business owners or further research online. Angel investors may frequent incubators, business conferences, leadership conferences, and expos. While looking for an angel investor, you should search your local area for business networking events and conferences. Join some start up clubs or apply to be in an entrepreneur incubator. Angel investors will visit these organizations to search for potential investments.

Things to keep in mind about Angel Investors:

❖ May be willing to allow you to build for long term success rather than a quick return.
❖ Possibly open to waiting longer on a return.
❖ Perhaps more open minded to make smaller investments.

■ Venture Capitalists

Venture capitalists are also wealthy individuals or organizations looking to invest in start-up companies but may be looking for a quicker return on their investment.

Institutional venture capital comes from professionally managed funds that have $25 million to $1 billion to invest in emerging growth companies. Unlike angel investors, venture capitalists have more control and ownership over the company and the decisions made and are usually more structured in their investments.

Blurred Lines

Actually, the line between angel investors and venture capitalists is becoming seemingly blurred when it comes to the need for a return. In the past, angel investors were more like mentors and were less concerned with a return. In recent years, both investors have become more concerned with the potential return on their investment.

As with angel investors, venture capitalists can exist as an established group or individuals. Some established venture capitalist firms include vSpring Capital of Salt Lake City, Utah, Illinois Ventures LLC of Chicago, Illinois, and Intel Capital of Santa Clara, California. Securing venture capitalists will take the same type of networking required with angel investors at business networking events and conferences.

Things to keep in mind about venture capitalists:

- ❖ Deal with larger investments
- ❖ Want to return a profit quickly
- ❖ Interested in businesses that can create a sizeable return

- ■ Crowd Funding

Crowd funding refers to a group of people who use small donations to fund an idea. The Jobs Act put in place by President Obama made it possible for everyday people to invest in businesses. These donations are used to fund company growth and the stake increases over time.

Well known crowd funders include:

- ✓ KickStarter
- ✓ Angel list
- ✓ IndieGoGo
- ✓ ProFounder
- ✓ MicroVentures

How To Appeal to Investors

There are several key factors that play a part in acquiring an investor. You should be familiar with these factors. When you approach a potential funder, know what type of businesses or industries they prefer to invest in and what key factors are most important to them. This information will help to increase your chances of convincing them to invest in your business. You want to make sure the investor has the interest and the time to spend on your type of business.

6 Things Investors Like To See

- ❖ **Demo** – You should do your best to have a working demo of the product or website to show how it works.
- ❖ **Customers** – If you have customers for validation, your idea will be more attractive to potential investors.
- ❖ **Location of Business** – Have you selected a location where there is a need for your product or service?
- ❖ **Stage of Development** – Will this be a start-up investment or is this a later round of funding?
- ❖ **Market Size** – What is the potential number of people that would actually use your product or service?

❖ **Competitive Advantage** – What is your position in the market compared to other businesses that offer similar products and services?

What Makes Your Idea Different

There are plenty of entrepreneurs looking for investors and investors hear a lot of pitches for companies. Make your big idea stand out from the crowd. You have to be able to set yourself apart from the others.

6 Ways to Make Yourself Standout to Investors

❖ **Strong elevator pitch** – Can you clearly explain your business in 60 seconds or less?

❖ **Testimonials** – Who will vouch for your product or service?
  o Industry experts
  o Established customers

❖ **Boot Strapping** – how far have you gotten without funding?

❖ **Management Team** – Do you have a strong and grounded management team?

❖ **Timeline** – What is your timeline before the initial investment can be returned?

❖ **Exit Strategy** – How will the arrangement end?

Things You Should Consider

Now, you know why you need funding, what funding options are available, what investors like to see, and how to stand apart from all of the entrepreneurs who are searching for money. To sum things up, there are some key points you should keep in the forefront of your mind.

❖ Specific criteria for each investor, be familiar with the investor and their points of interest
❖ Create a strong business model and demo
❖ Have defined milestones
❖ Strategy and direction of your business
❖ How much ownership are you willing to give away to an investor?
❖ How much funding do you need?

Begin with the end in mind

The last point that should be highlighted is the exit strategy. Young entrepreneur and author, Felecia Hatcher talks about this critical point in her blog post, "4 Things I Didn't Know About Investors Before I Took Their Money."

"The view of most investors is that there must be an identifiable exit route and an identifiable exit valuation before investing. Some of the best advice I received a few years ago was to determine if you are going to sell your business or keep it in the family for generations either way you need to treat your business like you are going to sell it because it gets you in a scalable mindset from day one."

Keep this in mind along your journey to funding your big idea. Investors will eventually want to cash out. Be clear from the beginning about what your plans are for exiting the business.

Launch Activity 4

What phase in your business will require funding?

_____

_____

_____

How can you grow your company through bootstrapping?

_____

_____

_____

How much money do you need and how soon?

_____

_____

_____

How will you use the funds to grow your business?

_____

_____

_____

Which type of investor is appropriate for your business?
Make a list of potential investors to contact.

_____

_____

_____

What is your elevator pitch for potential investors?

_____

_____

_____

What is your exit strategy?

_____

_____

_____

Chapter 5

Run a Lean Business

"EFFICIENCY IS DOING THINGS
RIGHT;

EFFECTIVENESS IS DOING THE
RIGHT THINGS."

-PETER DRUCKER

First of all, what *is* a "lean business?"

A lean business means you run your business to maximize your profit and customer experience while you minimize wasted money, time, and resources. You want to run your business with the least amount of waste and develop a system that keeps your costs down. In doing this, you have to maintain a welcoming customer experience. In a lean business, you are able to maintain a respectable level of service while reducing costs. Enhancing your customer experience is a very important operation that you want to directly relate to your cost. Remember your customers create your revenue.

Reality Check

It is very important to create lean business practices for your company but the most difficult and important step is to get people to adhere to those practices. Every business activity should have a policy or procedure but if no one is adhering to the procedures outlined, you have a problem. The lean practices must be enforced and become a part of the culture at your company. When you notice a part of your business that is not functioning properly or could be handled better, there are 7 questions you should ask yourself.

7 Questions to help you implement lean business practices

1. Do we have a policy and procedure for this business activity?
2. Is this the BEST policy and procedure for this part of the business?
3. Why are people not adhering to the policy or procedure?
4. Do we need further coaching or training on this policy/procedure?
5. Is the procedure too difficult?
6. Do we have the right people in place?
7. Is the correct equipment in place and is it functioning properly?

Secondly, why do you need to run a lean business?

Spending money in wasteful ways can ultimately result in the failure of your business. Also not being efficient with your time and resources will result in a slower rate of growth or possibly failure of your business. Focus on the long term success of the business. When you make better business decisions, you can move faster in the direction of having a prosperous business. You want to spend less money and get processes done faster and more efficiently.

Lean Finances

You need to make the best use of the money flowing into your business in order to generate greater profits. Wasteful spending can cause you to come up short for important operating expenses and purchases for growth. Keep focused on creating a positive cash flow of more revenue.

5 Tips to Run a Successful Lean Business

1. Set a Budget

- ❖ Delegate a certain amount of funds to a particular area of the business.
- ❖ Identify your fixed costs and variable costs and when they are due.

2. Reevaluate and Renegotiate

- ❖ Regularly take a look at every expense and ask if it is still relevant and needed for the businesses success.
- ❖ Eliminate unneeded expenses or reduce the amount you spend on them.
- ❖ Renegotiate deals with vendors or other service providers to save you money.

3. Consolidate Workspace

- ❖ Make the most of your money per square foot. Use office and production space wisely.

4. Shop Smarter

- ❖ Research products and vendors before making big purchases. Obtain multiple bids, at least three so you are able to bargain for cheaper prices. Consider using purchasing cards and places that offer rewards based on your spending.

5. Regulate Employee Costs

❖ Employee costs are usually the largest expense for a business. Wherever possible, find a way to substitute employees for automated services. Grocery stores now have "self check out" lanes which eliminates the need for extra cashiers. Or if you cannot eliminate the position completely, use technology to make the process quicker. This will result in more money made per hour you pay your employees.

Lean Culture and Mindset

The entire culture of your company should breathe lean practices. Incorporate lean practices down the stream so that middle managers are mindful and advocating a lean mindset to their direct reports. The lean mindset should then flow down to the entry level employees so they are mindful of how to best use time and resources. When you focus on being the most efficient at all times, it helps you to identify problems and solutions faster.

InBev, the Belgian-Brazilian global brewer is a prime of example of a business with a lean culture thoroughly engrained. The company is about protecting profitability and only doing what is necessary and most efficient for the company to have success. This mindset applies to all employees of the company no matter their rank or position. For example, senior level executives will stay at lower cost hotels and fly commercial when traveling compared to other global company's senior level executives who only fly private jets and stay at the most luxurious hotels.

In 2008, when InBev acquired Anhueser Busch they cut a lot of costs that were viewed as unnecessary and as inefficient uses of resources. An Anhueser Busch employee that was around prior to the InBev take over once told a story of how at one corporate building there was a floor with three huge offices, one for the ceo, cfo, and coo. The floor was like a museum with historic company items that belonged to founder Adolphus Busch. It was a floor full of A-B tradition. InBev quickly recognized this as poorly utilized space and consolidated the workspace by taking museum-like offices and transforming them into smaller cubicles in order to accommodate more employees. The Anhueser Busch employee said there are now over 75 people working in a space where there was once only three. Applying world class efficiency is a way of life now at the newly formed Anhueser Busch InBev.

The lean culture should stay with you throughout the life of your business. Think *lean while* you are small, and think *lean* when your idea grows to be big. You should always operate at the highest level of efficiency.

5S Methodology

5S is a workplace organization method that will help you to implement lean practices. It comes from the five Japanese words: seiri, seiton, seiso, seiketsu, and shitsuke. Translated to English you get sorting, set in order, systematic cleaning (shine), standardize, and self discipline.

Sorting

In this phase you want to eliminate all unnecessary tools or parts. Only keep your required tools and material and get rid of what is not needed. Prioritize things based on how often you use them and keep them in easily accessible places. Everything else should be stored or thrown away.

Set in Order

Arrange the work, workers, equipment, parts, and instructions in a way that the work flow is free of any waste through the task or labor involved. If applied correctly, this step will eliminate a large portion of the non-value added time in your work.

Systematic Cleaning

Keep the workspace and all equipment clean and organized. At the end of each work session the work area should be cleaned and prepared for the next user.

Standardize

Ensure uniform processes and setups throughout the operation to promote interchangeability.

Self Discipline

Ensure disciplined adherence to rules and procedures to prevent backsliding. This may be the most important step.

Lean Benchmarks

Set benchmarks. Be the best in the industry and the most profitable in your market. If everyone in the industry is growing, you want to grow at a faster rate. Alternatively if everyone in the industry is losing, you want to lose less.

You should constantly evaluate lean practices and make sure your implementations are being followed throughout the company. Be sure to track for a positive effect on any changes made. The key to a successful lean business is that the mindset is continuous. You want it to flow through all processes and people in the company. It's not a short-term goal but a lifestyle cultural engraining of the business.

Think Lean!

Launch Activity 5

1) Identify a part of your business that is not functioning properly or could be handled better. Answer the **7 Questions to help you implement lean business practices** in the beginning of the chapter to find a solution.

_____

_____

_____

_____

_____

_____

2) Review the **5 Tips to Run a Successful Lean Business** and write down how you will apply it to your business.

_____

_____

_____

_____

_____

_____

3) Review the *5S Methodology* and write down how you will apply it to your business.

_____

_____

_____

_____

_____

_____

_____

4) Create 3 lean bench marks for your company.

_____

_____

_____

_____

_____

_____

5) Prepare a meeting about the lean practices that your company will implement and share with your team members.

_____

_____

_____

_____

_____

_____

_____

Chapter 6

The Social Media Advantage

"MARKETING IS NO LONGER ABOUT THE STUFF THAT YOU MAKE,

BUT ABOUT THE STORIES YOU TELL."

-SETH GODIN

Importance of social media

Social networks are not just places to post your latest photos and vent your societal frustrations. As you launch your big idea, you can use social networks as a free and convenient marketing tool to reach a broad audience at once. You can connect and build relationships with your customers. Social media can be used to broadcast promotions and services on Facebook and Twitter or even make online videos with YouTube and Instagram to advertise your business. It's the fastest way to share and update information.

It's important for every business to integrate social networking into their overall business strategy. Not only are business owners of today *expected* to have a social media presence, but it enables you to connect with current and potential customers in a variety of ways. A study from socialmediatoday.com found that 90% of purchases are subject to consumer influence. This means that more than likely the product you are selling could benefit from a quality social networking program. People talking about your product or service on social media sites could create more customers from their posts and comments. Keep in mind this works both ways when customers are satisfied and when they are not so happy with your service. You want to keep the comments positive so be sure to do outstanding work.

SOCIAL ENGAGEMENT

The biggest goal of social networking is creating social engagement between your business and customers. It is not having 100,000 random followers on Twitter; instead it is about creating an active audience of brand advocates. If you focus your attention on creating a genuine following you will have an audience that will help to spread the message about your product or service. Remember the following message as you read about best practices for different social media outlets. In this case, quality is ranked higher than quantity.

Best Practices for Businesses and Social Networking

❖ Facebook

✓ Over 1 billion active users
✓ Largest Social Network
✓ Must have a business presence on Facebook

Facebook Best Practices:

1. Create a Business Page
   a. Reach your audience with a level of engagement.

Everyone who likes your posts, comments on your status, or interacts with you on Facebook is a potential customer.

2. Manage your profile
   a. Ensure company information is current and up-to-date.
   b. Facebook will drive potential customers to your website. Maintain accurate information on your company's website.

3. Be Active. Comment on other people's posts.
   a. Try to reach as many people as possible for more exposure.

4. For every 10 posts that are not related to your business, there should be at least 1 business-related post.
   a. Invite people to learn your personality as well as the nature of your business.

5. Limit negative and extra personal posts.
   a. Remember, you control the image you portray to your customers and potential customers.

6. Keep posts short, between 100-140 characters.
   a. Studies show short posts receive more activity.
   b. Short posts are also simple to cross reference on other sites like Twitter.

7. Incorporate pictures and videos whenever possible.
   a. Pictures and videos will help generate engagement and give customers a visual element of your product experience.

8. Create groups.
   a. You can reach a particular audience by creating groups and targeting those individuals.

9. Create a custom link shortener for your website.
   a. Custom short domains keep your brand front and center. Your audience trusts them above generic link shorteners. New York Times uses http://nyti.ms/news instead of http://bit.ly/jfonUf

b. Mobile users may be discouraged in following the link because they are unsure of what site they are being directed to visit.

c. To see an example visit http://www.enterprise.bitly.com/

10. Post during peak times for maximum engagement.
    a. To get to the top of the timeline, post between 1pm – 4pm.
    b. The most active time is Wednesday at 3pm.
    c. Dead times are before 8am and after 8pm.
    d. Better engagement occurs toward the weekend, like Thursday and Friday.
    e. Slower interaction days are Monday and Tuesday.

11. Do not over post and kill previous posts.
    a. The average life of a post, the time it remains on the newsfeed, is about 3 hours.

12. Use action words.
    a. Certain words generate engagement such as:
       (1) Comment
       (2) Post
       (3) Tell us
       (4) Take
       (5) Submit
       (6) Like

13. Ask questions.
    a. Avoid the question "Why?"
    b. Instead, ask the what, where, when, should, would.

14. Create contests.
    a. Invite followers to participate in contests, naming a winner.

Facebook is an easy site to promote your business. Be careful of being overly aggressive and personal but remember to post during peak times and engage your Facebook friends in the activity on your page with contests, campaigns, and giveaways.

❖ Twitter
✓ Over 500 million active users
✓ Easier than Facebook
✓ Enables business to be searchable

Twitter Best Practices:

1. Create a business profile and biography.
   a. Include keywords in your biography that define your product or service.
   b. People will be able to search keywords and locate your business on Twitter.

2. Use hashtags.
   a. For example, if you own a Sports Bar, during the big game, tweet with the hashtags #superbowl or #biggame or #NFLplayoffs.
3. Use mentions.
   a. Expand your network by integrating more people and followers.

4. Organize followers into lists.
   a. By using a list, you can target potential customers and reach other business partners.
   b. Example lists could be suppliers, competitors, or potential customers in neighboring suburb.

5. Schedule Tweets.
   a. In case you forget to Tweet, schedule tweets for a particular time of day.

6. Frequently update profile picture.
   a. You want to keep your page fresh and current.

7. Create Twitter Landing Page on your website.
   a. Place a link from your website that will lead visitors from your website to your Twitter profile.

8. Be active.
   a. Engage your followers. Make sure your presence is known.

  b. Ask people to follow you on your website and other social networks.

  c. Follow your customers.

 9. Add photos and links to Tweets.

  a. Attract attention to your profile with interesting Tweets.

 10. Tweet about current events.

  a. Other people will notice your Tweet on a trending topic and possibly spark an interest in your business.

Keep in mind that the more you tweet, the more followers you get so tweet, tweet, and tweet. Twitter is an easy and laid back site where you can easily gain exposure and develop a good reputation for your business.

❖ Pinterest

✓ Third largest social network
✓ Fastest stand alone site to reach 10 million visitors
✓ Generates more traffic than YouTube, Google +, and Linked In all together

Pinterest Best Practices:

1. Use original pictures of products.

  a. Put links to your website so visitors can make purchases.

  b. People prefer original content.

2. Pin other people's content.
   a. Repin their content to one of your boards.

3. Use "Pin It" Button on your website.
   a. Drive interest to your Pinterest account to see more of your original products and services.
4. Run competitions and giveaways.

5. Create a guest pinner board.
   a. Allow fans to repin photos and videos that are related to your business.

6. Create a catalog.
   a. Create a board and put pictures of the board that have to do with your services. Also include prices of the products to help drive business.
   b. Nordstrom is known for linking items on their board to their products.

7. Create a Coupon Board.
   a. Promote discounts and savings for your customers.

Pinterest is a photo-sharing social network where it's convenient to create boards and post pictures. It's a very easy way to create a personality for your business. We have a board for the Best of St. Louis, where we highlight subjects that we think is important to the city like the

Cardinals or the arch. We also have an art board where we pin famous works of art. Those boards help show our personality but we also have an auto detail board which is directly related to our business, where we highlight nice cars and cars we have serviced.

❖ Instagram
- ✓ Mobile based network
- ✓ Instagram reports it has 90 million users
- ✓ Reports of 40 million pictures are shared each day

Instagram Best Practices:

1. Create a business account.

2. Post before and after pictures.
   a. For example, show pictures of the product from its fabrication to finished product.

3. Post pictures or videos of people using your product.

4. Use the video feature to create a different visual experience for followers.

5. Post pictures of your product or service.
   a. If you're a clothing business: Show pictures of your items for sale, new

products, graphics of upcoming sales, or employees providing that service.

6. Use hastags.
    a. Users from around the world can follow you.
    b. Sometimes Showroom Shine Express Detailing uses the hastags #autodetailing, #carwash, #Mercedes,"#carguys," and people from across the globe in Germany and Russia searching for different hashtags end up liking the photos.

❖ LinkedIn

✓ Over 135 million members in over 200 countries
✓ Business professional atmosphere
✓ More than a place to upload resumes

LinkedIn Best Practices:

1. Make the most out of your profile.
    a. Great place for business to business marketing, especially for a particular industry.

2. Conduct market research, looking for competitors, industry standards and expectations.

3. Completely fill in all fields.

4. Change URL to business name rather than LinkedIn generated number.

5. Look at upgrades.

6. Use LinkedIn search feature.
    a. Find potential business contacts and leads.
    b. Look for people to connect with in different industries and with different levels of expertise.

7. Use what you already have.
    a. Utilize the LinkedIn apps and blogs.
    b. Link your blog, profile, and other content to your LinkedIn profile.

8. Be mindful of how business will be portrayed.
    a. What you put on Facebook or Twitter may not be acceptable on LinkedIn; LinkedIn is a more professional environment.

❖ Google+

✓ Over 400 million members
✓ About 100 million monthly active members
✓ A unique way to interact with customers

Google+ Best Practices:

1. Create circles.

      a. Instead of groups and lists, like Facebook and Twitter, use circles to reach a particular audience.

2. Define the information you share.
      a. Target information to a particular group.

3. Be conscious of key words.
      a. Use keywords in "About" section to generate more traffic.
      b. Use words you want to rank high in relating to your customers.

4. Add links throughout your page.

This social network will benefit your business in creating more search engine results. Most of your traffic comes from Google and having this profile makes it easier for your business to be found.

Launch Activity 6

Which social networks will your business use?

_____

_____

_____

_____

_____

_____

Setup your complete profile for the social networks your business will use.

Who will manage your social networks?

_____

_____

_____

_____

_____

How often will you post on each network?

_____

_____

_____

_____

_____

What type of content will you post that is consistent with your brand?

_____

_____

_____

_____

_____

What will you do to create engagement with your social media followers?

_____

_____

_____

_____

CHAPTER 7

DEVELOP A WINNING BUSINESS MODEL

"NEWSPAPERS WITH DECLINING CIRCULATIONS CAN COMPLAIN ALL THEY WANT ABOUT THEIR READERS AND EVEN SAY THEY HAVE NO TASTE. BUT YOU WILL STILL GO OUT OF BUSINESS OVER TIME. A NEWSPAPER IS NOT A PUBLIC TRUST. IT HAS A BUSINESS MODEL THAT EITHER WORKS OR IT DOESN'T."
-MARC ANDREESEN

Developing a Business Idea

Before you can develop a winning business model, you must have an idea for your business. You want to determine what product or service your company will offer, and in turn, what the product experience feels and looks like. You need to understand your potential customers and what problems your business will solve for them.

Think of what you are most passionate about and how that passion aligns with your skill set. You need to find your niche and use it to fill a void that currently exists. Talk to other business organizations, schools, or entrepreneurs who may be in search of a business partner.

Be sure your idea is in line with the trends and technologies of the time. For example, Groupon is the new way to coupon. It's in line with the ease and convenience for mobile users and it's beneficial to its customers.

• Developing a Winning Business Model

Let's start by defining a business plan versus a business model.

*Business **plan**:* Spend time researching inside the building versus in the market place to see if your idea is viable. The plan is very rigid and not flexible, not allowing you to change course as you gather more information.

*Business **model**:* Identify and define assumptions about your business idea. Conduct field tests on operations, how customers receive your business idea, and other ideas you want to implement within your company.

In a business model, you are able to learn what really works and it also allows you to "pivot" on the realities of your research. The ultimate goal of a business model is to validate your business idea by initiating lean start up practices. That way you are more focused on understanding your customers and what is acceptable in the market instead of potentially wasting funds on an impractical idea.

There are 9 short steps to developing a winning business model.

Take time to answer these questions about your big idea and you will end up with a better understanding of what it will take to succeed in the market place.

1. **Understand your value proposition**

    o   What is your value proposition?

    o   What value are you offering to your customers?

    o   What problems are you solving?

Your contribution needs to be clear. Young entrepreneur Candera Walker's natural hair and skin care business, L.A.C.E. Natural is clear that its goal is to offer quality products with the best ingredients to promote healthy hair of all types and skin. As she prepared to launch her big idea she kept her value proposition in mind as she created her product line to sell to customers.

Potential Value Propositions

- Outstanding service

- Convenience

- Affordable pricing

- Personalization and customization

- Status

2. Customer Segments

You need to understand how customers are segmented and determine which segments you are trying to target. The natural hair care company has a specific customer segment for different products. Some products are focused on men, women, or children. Know who you want to reach with your product or service.

o   What are your customer segments?

o Who are you creating this product or service for?

o Is it a particular niche or a broad customer base?

Potential Customer Segments

- Niche

- Mass market

- Demographics (Age, Gender, Economic status)

3. Customer Connections

Constantly evaluate if your method of connecting with your customer is relevant and helping your customers to understand the value your product or service provides. With the natural hair care company, they could use Google Ad words online which leads to their website to purchase the supplies. Now, their methods of connection are integrated. There could also be a physical store front

location, which provides more than one means of
connecting with their potential and current customers.

- How will you reach your customers?
- How do each 1 of your segments want to be reached?
- Which ways have worked best?
- How is your business integrated with your customer's routine?
- Which ways are cost efficient?
- How are customers purchasing your product?

Potential Customer Connections

- Online
- Storefront
- E-Blasts
- Retail
- Wholesale

4. Customer Relationships

- o What type of relationships does each of your customer segments expect?

- o How much time and money will it take to create and maintain those relationships?

- o What relationships have you already established?

Understand each segment is different and will require more or less attention depending on the segment. Be conscious of those expectations and maintain that level of interaction throughout your relationship with these customers. For example, L.A.C.E Natural may have to spend more time soliciting salon or store owners, to get her products on the shelves.

Potential Customer Expectations

- Personal service
- Automation

- Self-service

- Community involvement

- Personalization

5. Revenue Stream

Understand what value your customers are willing to pay. Determine how the pricing in each revenue stream will be established – fixed or dynamic pricing, based on volume, negotiable, etc. As a business owner, understand the wants and needs of your customers, in order to gage what services or products they'd be willing to pay for.

o   How do you generate revenue?

o   What are all the ways you could bring money into your business?

o   How much does each stream contribute to the total revenue?

o   What do your customers currently pay for?

o   What methods are available for payment?

o   Which ways do your customers prefer to pay?

Potential Revenue Streams

- Sale of product or service

- Service Fee

- Rental Fee

- Advertising Fee

- Subscription Fee

- Licensing

6. Key Resources

Understand what resources you will need to execute

each phase of this model. For example, the natural hair care

company needed an e-commerce website built to reach

their online customer segment. Determining your resources

is an important step toward implementing your model.

o What key resources does your Value Proposition require?

o What key resources do your Customer Segments require?

o What key resources do your Customer Connections require?

o What key resources do your Customer Relationships require?

o What key resources does your Revenue Stream require?

Potential Key Resources

- Financial capital
- Human capital
- Intellectual capital
- Patents and copyrights
- Property

7. Key Activities

It is important to understand the key activities necessary for each phase of the model. One key activity for L.A.C.E. Natural would include networking with customers at trade shows as a part of Customer Connections. This networking could introduce current and potential customers to new products and services the company offers.

- o What key activities does your Value Proposition require?

- o What key activities do your Customer Segments require?

- o What key activities do your Customer Connections require?

- o What key activities do your Customer Relationships require?

- o What key activities does your Revenue Stream require?

Potential Key Activities

- Networking

- Productivity

- Problem-solving skills

- Critical Thinking

- Brainstorming

- Platform

8. Key Partners

Understand that partnerships are important to a business because by yourself you cannot perform every activity necessary to run your business, or you cannot supply every need. Relationships help you to reduce risks and manage your business more efficiently. The natural hair and skin care company needs suppliers to provide the products they sell. Without the supplier, the business cannot operate.

o Who are the vital partners that you may need in order to have a successful business?

o What resources do we get from each partner?

o What activities do those partners perform?

Potential Partners

- Suppliers

- Vendors

- Employees

- Financial Institutions

- Investors

9. Cost Structure

Understand and determine if your business is more cost driven or more value driven. If it is more cost driven, you are more concerned about the price instead of the service you provide. If it is more value driven then you are competing on service and not price. In a value driven situation the price will be higher.

- o What are your most important costs?

- o What is most expensive?

- o How much do your resources, activities, and partners cost?

Potential Costs

- Fixed Costs

- Supplies

- Utilities

- Rent

- Material

- Labor

Now your business model is complete. It will help you understand important pieces needed for success and allow you to test your business idea. The overall goal is to help you get your business started in the leanest fashion with real-world data from focus groups, potential customers, and existing customers to support your thought process.

While going through the module, you will probably run into some areas that are not realistic and some ideas that are not feasible. In these instances, you must be willing to pivot and change the course of the model. The best part about this model is it allows for pivoting and you are not locked into one set way of implementing your idea. The model warrants you to go back and adjust any phase that is not sustainable.

Using this model, you can create a viable business framework and work through the process, making changes as necessary. It's better to find out problem areas during the testing phase. This way you have not over invested time, money, or energy into the idea that may require you to go back to the drawing board. The alternative is to launch full scale and find out your failures in a few years. This is what we want to avoid by using this process.

Remember the key word in this model is *winning;* develop

a *winning* business model for your big idea.

Launch Activity 7

Identify and define assumptions about your business idea. Conduct field tests on operations, how do customers receive your business idea and other ideas you want to implement within your company?

_____

_____

_____

_____

_____

_____

Review the 9 steps to developing a winning business model. Write down your answers to all the questions that apply to your business.

_____

_____

_____

_____

_____

30 Days To Launch

It is important to note before you get started that this 30 day guide is not intended to be a get rich scheme. The purpose of putting it in a 30 day format is to help you conquer any entrepreneurship paralysis and keep you focused. Each day represents a different task to complete that can be implemented within a day. Some task may require more time or less time based on external factors. However, by focusing on these 30 tasks by the end of the 30 days you should have a successful foundation to launch your big idea! Now let's get started.

Day 1: Choose an idea for a product or service.

Day 2: Decide who startup team members will be and identity responsibilities and roles.

Day 3: Determine your value proposition.

Day 4: Choose name and vision statement for your business.

Day 5: Define your Customer Segments.

Day 6: Establish Customer Connections.

Day 7: Classify Customer Relationships.

Day 8: Determine Revenue Streams.

Day 9: Identify Key Resources.

Day 10: Determine Key Activities.

Day 11: Identify Key Partners.

Day 12: Evaluate Cost Structure and potential profit margins.

Day 13: Choose an accountant and an attorney for financial and legal advice.

Day 14: Determine legal business structure and ownership distribution.

Day 15: Develop partnership agreement.

Day 16: Incorporate your business and apply for federal tax identification number (EIN), and state identification numbers if required. Research to see if your city and/or county require any licenses or permits to operate your type of business.

Day 17: Open a bank account and purchase business insurance.

Day 18: Choose and purchase domain name. Find hosting site. Set up telephone and internet access.

Day 19: Find office space in desired location.

Day 20: Find platform, developers, graphic designers that will work for your business.

Day 21: Begin logo, website, and print designs.

Day 22: Create social pages for your business. (Facebook, Twitter, Pinterest, Instagram, YouTube, Google+, etc)

Day 23: Find a focus group of 5 people from your defined customer segments to test out your product or service.

Day 24: Survey the focus group and evaluate their customer experience.

Day 25-27: Decide if any changes should be made to your business model. Refer back to day's 5-12 to pivot. Take time to enhance the business model based on the results from your focus group. You want to make sure your product or service is ready to hit the market.

Day 28: Plan your grand opening/Launch event.

Day 29: Create buzz about your event through press releases, e-blasts, invites, and word of mouth.

Day 30: Launch ....Sell, Sell, Sell in the days and months to come.

YOUNG

ENTREPRENEUR

RESOURCES

NETWORKING

-**TheYoungInc:**theyounginc.com

(Social network designed to connect entrepreneurs from around the world. Supporting them with business news, articles, blogs, forums, interviews, and templates.)

-**Twitter:** www.twitter.com

-**Facebook:** www.facebook.com

-**LinkedIn:** www.linkedin.com

-**Instagram:** www.instagram.com

-**Youtube:** www.youtube.com

-**Google+:** www.google.com/+

-**Pinterest:** www.pinterest.com

-**Vine:** www.vine.co

-**Tumblr:** www.tumblr.com

-**Youngentrepreneur.com:** www.youngentrepreneur.com

-**Partner Up:** www.partnerup.com

-**Young Success Network:** www.ysn.com

General Business Resources

-**Score:** www.score.org/young

-**Allbusiness.com:** www.allbusiness.com

-**Startup Nation:** www.startupnation.com

-**Entrepreneur Magazine:** www.entrepreneur.com

Marketing Resources

-**Constant Contact:** www.constantcontact.com

-**Got Print:** www.gotprint.com

-**Business Marketing Assoc.:** www.marketing.org

-**Mail Chimp:** www.mailchimp.com

-**Sales Force:** www.salesforce.com

Accounting Resources

-**QuickBooks:** www.quickbooks.com

-**IRS:** www.irs.com

-**Peach Tree:** www.peachtree.com

-**Fresh Books:** www.freshbooks.com

-**Turbo Tax:** www.turbotax.com

Human Resources

-**National HR Assoc:** www.humanresources.org

-**Society for HR Management:** www.shrm.org

Inventors Resources

-**U.S. Patent and Trademark Office:** www.uspto.gov

-**Ideatango:** www.ideatango.com

-**Invent Help:** www.inventhelp.com

Business Legal Resource

-**Legal Zoom:** www.legalzoom.com

Web Domain Names

GoDaddy.com: www.godaddy.com

Register.com: www.register.com

Website Builders and Themes

Wix.com: www.wix.com

Weebly: www.weebly.com

WooThemes: www.woothemes.com

Site Point: www.sitepoint.com

Blogging

Blogger: www.blogger.com

Word Press: www.wordpress.com

www.wordpress.org

App Building Resources

Main Street Apps: www.mainstreet-apps.com

AppMakr: www.appmakr.com

App Machine: www.appmachine.com

Virtual Assistants and Freelancers

Elance: www.elance.com

Fiverr: www.fiverr.com

99Designs: www.99designs.com

Freelancer: www.freelancer.com

Odesk.com: www.odesk.com

Venture Capital

Capital Vector: www.capitalvector.com

National Venture Capital Association: www.nvca.com

Venture Capital & Investors: www.fundingpost.com

Crowd Funding

Kickstarter.com: www.kickstarter.com

Lending Club: www.lendingclub.com

Peer Lending: www.peerlendingnetwork.com

Prosper.com: www.prosper.com

Gofundme: www.crowdfunding.com

Government Grants

Grants.gov: www.grants.gov

US Gov. Grants: www.usgovernmentgrants.org

Publicity

Prweb.com: www.prweb.com

HARO: www.haro.com

The Publicity Hound: www.publicityhound.com

Loans

Small Business Administration: www.sba.gov

Green Business Resources

-Green Biz: www.greenbiz.com

-Green Dreams: www.greendreams.com

-Greenopia: www.greenopia.com

Minority Business Resource

Minority Business Development Agency: www.mbda.gov

Woman Business Resources

-Women Business Support Network: www.wbsnonline.org

-Advancing Women: www.advancingwomen.com